YOUR KNOWLEDGE HAS VALUE

- We will publish your bachelor's and master's thesis, essays and papers

- Your own eBook and book - sold worldwide in all relevant shops

- Earn money with each sale

Upload your text at www.GRIN.com
and publish for free

Bibliographic information published by the German National Library:

The German National Library lists this publication in the National Bibliography; detailed bibliographic data are available on the Internet at http://dnb.dnb.de .

This book is copyright material and must not be copied, reproduced, transferred, distributed, leased, licensed or publicly performed or used in any way except as specifically permitted in writing by the publishers, as allowed under the terms and conditions under which it was purchased or as strictly permitted by applicable copyright law. Any unauthorized distribution or use of this text may be a direct infringement of the author s and publisher s rights and those responsible may be liable in law accordingly.

Imprint:

Copyright © 2018 GRIN Verlag
Print and binding: Books on Demand GmbH, Norderstedt Germany
ISBN: 9783668690691

This book at GRIN:

https://www.grin.com/document/417971

Kathleen Jackson

The connection of management concepts to the Capsim simulation

GRIN Verlag

GRIN - Your knowledge has value

Since its foundation in 1998, GRIN has specialized in publishing academic texts by students, college teachers and other academics as e-book and printed book. The website www.grin.com is an ideal platform for presenting term papers, final papers, scientific essays, dissertations and specialist books.

Visit us on the internet:

http://www.grin.com/

http://www.facebook.com/grincom

http://www.twitter.com/grin_com

Kathleen Jackson
Simulation Reflection
2018

SIMULATION REFLECTION

Table of Contents

Instructions: 2
Selected Responses 4
   Strategy 4
   Functions of Management 5
   Goals and Objectives 6
   Benchmarking 7
   Decisions 8
   Reflection 9
References 12

List of Tables

Table 1: Relevant Literature for additional reading 10

SIMULATION REFLECTION

Instructions:

Answer each question to the best of your ability.
Use proper English – APA Style version 6.0.
Single-space your responses.
Keep your essay responses to no more than two (2) pages per individual question response.
Incorporate literature references you deem appropriate.
Begin each question on a separate page. Put the question at the top of the page.
Include an automated table of contents.
Include a cover page.
Include a reference list (APA Style).
Include all materials in a single document.
Submit both a physical copy and an electronic copy.
After instructor review and approval, submit for publication.
You must do questions 11 and 12.
Answer any five (5) from the remaining questions (including 11 & 12).

1. This semester, our simulation introduced the concept of strategy. Please define the term strategy, and discuss how it affects corporate management and leadership.
2. Our simulation involves direct application of the primary functions of management. Please identify and discuss examples of each primary management function within the context of your simulation.
3. The simulation involves considerations of both goals and objectives. Please define both terms and delineate their commonness and differences. Within your discussion, please explain how you have incorporated both goals and objectives within your simulation.
4. Our simulation integrates the primary domains of business administration ranging from accounting to forecasting. Please identify and explain three domains within the context of the simulation.
5. The simulation necessitates considerations of contingencies. Please define and explain the basic concept of contingency planning. Within your response, please discuss how you incorporated the basic concept of contingency planning.
6. The simulation necessitates considerations of benchmarking. Please define the basic concept of benchmarking, and discuss how it is applicable within the context of your simulation.
7. Please identify and explain three instances of marginal or poor performance that your team experienced during the simulation. How do you believe your team can rectify the unsatisfactory performance, and incite change toward generating positive outcomes within the simulation? What process improvement methods and maturity models are available for improving your performance?
8. Please identify and explain three instances of good or superior performance that your team experienced during the simulation. How do you believe your team can maintain the acceptable performance toward generating positive outcomes within the simulation?
9. The simulation necessitates a variety of strategic, tactical, and operational decisions. Identify and explain an example of each type of decision that you have implemented within the simulation.
10. The simulation necessitated communication and information sharing within the context of running the technology company. Please discuss how you integrated communication and the intelligence cycle when experiencing the simulation.
11. **Required:** How would you assess your performance this term throughout the course of the simulation? What opportunities for performance improvement do you see regarding your simulation experience? How do you plan to take advantage of these opportunities to generate positive outcomes within the simulation? Refer to your answers from the preceding questions to support your answer. Include literature as necessary.
12. **Required:** Include a literature table that incorporates the basic topic areas that you used throughout the course. Within each topic area, include a minimum of four literature references that supported your discussions. Include these items in your reference listing. A good way to earn the points is to finish the

literature table that we started this semester using the instructor's template. You may add additional references beyond those in the template to satisfy this requirement.

Your submission format should be presented in the following format:

1. Cover page
2. Contents
3. Question sheet – this document.
4. Your Selected Question Responses – start the response to each question on a new page. Place the question at the top of the page. Your responses should be a minimum of one page, but no more than two pages. Answer the questions in numerical order.
5. Question #11 and your response.
6. Question #12 and your response (add your discovered references to the table).
7. References (add your discovered references to the reference template).

Selected Responses

Strategy

This semester, our simulation introduced the concept of strategy. Please define the term strategy, and discuss how it affects corporate management and leadership.

This semester, we utilized the Capsim simulation which introduced the concept of strategy. This simulation allowed us to experience what it's like to manage a business. It allowed us to be involved in business by exposing us to concepts and terminology in a simulated environment. This simulation required a great deal of thought, planning, trial and error, and strategy. There were several different tabs, such as pricing, operational, and product, each calling for a different method of filling them out. Strategy was one of the most vital elements used in progressing through the simulation. Simply entering numbers and values would have led to less than sufficient outcomes. The class had to formulate strategies to be successful and meet objectives. This concept is true in the real world as well, as strategy plays a great role in corporate management and leadership.

Before discussing how strategy is intertwined with business and corporate management, it is important to first understand exactly what it means. Strategy is a method or plan chosen to bring about a desired future, such as achievement of a goal or solution to a problem, and strategic management applies this concept (How Has This Term Impacted Your Life?, n.d.). It is an organization's long-term scope, which brings about an advantage through its use of materials. It allows market demand and stakeholder's expectations to be met (Riley, n.d.).

Corporate management, the process of leading, administrating, and directing a company, goes hand in hand with leadership and varies based on the company's overall strategy (What is Corporate Management?, n.d.). Separating facets of a business into smaller categories such as pricing, products, and operations, not only makes processes much smoother, it also requires different strategies for each one. The methods a company chooses to use affects corporate management and leadership. The way it operates determines how management directs staff and employees. Certain strategies require different things and responsibilities from the workers in order to meet long term goals. Depending on the strategy, managers and company owners must choose how strict or lenient they will be on their employees and even increase or decrease their workloads. Also, communication processes must be adjusted based on strategy. Company leaders must understand how to effectively communicate with people like investors, stakeholders, and employee. A successful leader must know how to adjust based on who he or she is talking to and must communicate according to the company's strategy (Anthony, 2018).

Functions of Management

Our simulation involves direct application of the primary functions of management. Please identify and discuss examples of each primary management function within the context of your simulation.

While progressing through our simulation, we were required to carry out the primary functions of management. The functions of management include planning, organizing, leading, and controlling, and each of them are connected in some way (Principles of Management, n.d.). Each of these functions can be found in a majority of, if not all, companies and businesses. The simulation mimicked a realistic company in a market situation; therefore, it comes as no surprise that it required us to apply them.

Planning refers to defining performance goals for the organization and determining what actions and resources are needed to achieve these goals. By planning, a company is able to forecast future states of the organization and determine how to reach that state (Principles of Management, 2015). The class did a great deal of planning within the simulation. Much time and thought had to be spent things on setting prices and similar things before submission for the next round. Without planning, the results would have been insufficient.

Organizing can be defined as forming an organizational structure and assigning tasks to employees to reach goals and objectives. Usually, it is outlined graphically by charts that represent the chain of command within a company or business. Decisions regarding the structures are called organizational design decisions (Principles of Management, 2015). In our simulation, we used the spreadsheets for each category. They had charts, tables, and graphs that we used for making decisions. Also, in the beginning of the year, we assigned a leader who then assigned tasks to the rest of the class. These are all instances of organizing that we used in the simulation.

As stated in Principles of Management, leading encompasses the "sources of influence" that are used to get a certain result from others (2015). Effective leaders should be positive and uplifting, and willing to show effort to reach company goals (Principles of Management, 2015). Our leader exhibited these skills during the simulation and was relatively enthusiastic throughout.

Controlling is making sure that the team does not stray from company expectations and standards (Principles of Management, 2015). There are three steps in the control process. The first step is to establish standards. Next, performance must be assessed based on those standards. The last step is correcting any changes from the set standards and plans (Merchant, n.d.). Controlling was used during our simulation. When each round begins, we set a goal for the results we wanted to see. Once we carried out the necessary steps that we hoped would lead us to reaching the goals, we submitted. We checked to see how we did and tried to adjust so we could avoid the same result next round.

Goals and Objectives

The simulation involves considerations of both goals and objectives. Please define both terms and delineate their commonness and differences. Within your discussion, please explain how you have incorporated both goals and objectives within your simulation.

During the simulation, we set various goals and objectives. While many use the two interchangeably, they have their differences. Before discussing their commonness and differences, it is important to have an understanding of their basic definitions. A goal is a desired result or outcome to which efforts are directed. It provides a broad, general outcome. An example of a goal could be a company saying that it wants to become the leader of its market. An objective sets a measurable target outcome so that a strategy can be formed around it. Objectives are steps a business takes to reach a desired outcome (Ghanbari, 2014). An example of an objective could be a company saying that it wants to increase its share by 20% by the end of the year. Objectives and goals have things in common, but also have distinct differences.

Objectives and goals are similar in that they both give the company something to work towards. Effort and time will be dedicated to reach them. Businesses can have more than one of each. However, it is important to note that there are aspects that set them apart from one another. One aspect is one is broad, and the other specific. A goal lacks measurement, while an objective is measurable in specific. Further, an objective is a measurable step an organization takes to reach goals (Ghanbari, 2014). Another difference is that a goal can be categorized as long term and objectives as short term. Goals are typically based on ideas, and objectives are based on things that are more factual and concrete (Morrison, 2011).

In our time in the simulation, the class had both goals and objectives. At the start of the simulation, we stated that we wanted to be highly ranked at the close of the simulation. This is a goal. After setting this goal, we had to form specific objectives to reach this goal. Each week we set objectives for things such as issuing a certain amount of stock, producing a desired amount of goods, and producing new products. As previously mentioned, goals are broad, and objectives are specific. This was evident to us while setting ours.

Benchmarking

The simulation necessitates considerations of benchmarking. Please define the basic concept of benchmarking and discuss how it is applicable within the context of your simulation.

Benchmarking has played a huge role in our simulation. Benchmarking is the process of comparing organizations to other companies and competitors in the industry or market. This allows business to recognize areas of improvement, opportunities to lower costs, raise earnings, and improve customer loyalty. It is important for companies to benchmark because it allows them to improve internally while keeping an eye on evolving methods of the competition. Businesses are able to gather data about themselves at various points and find gaps that they can fill. Also, they assess themselves in relation to competitors in order to attain a competitive edge and to get more of an understanding of their methods. Sometimes a company will choose to use strategic benchmarking or comparing its performance to that of the best. This goes outside of the bounds of their own industry (Reh, 2017).

During our simulation, we participated in a great deal of benchmarking. On a few of the spreadsheets, charts were provided to show how other companies were performing in our market alongside our own. As previously mentioned, this allows companies to find areas of improvement. This is true for our simulation. We viewed how the other products and companies were doing and adjusted values on our spreadsheets to improve. Also, we used benchmarking when we looked at the rankings of other institutions. Our ranking showed that while we were performing better than some, we still had room for much improvement.

Decisions

The simulation necessitates a variety of strategic, tactical, and operational decisions. Identify and explain an example of each type of decision that you have implemented within the simulation.

Since the simulation mimicked a realistic company, decisions that would typically be made in the real world had to be made during the simulation. A decision is making a choice with intent to direct efforts toward reach a desired state. Once a decision is made, materials are used to get to said state (Developing People Through Business Case Studies, n.d.). There are three types of decisions in particular that had to be made. They are strategic, tactical, and operational decisions.

Strategic decisions are those that are long-term and made by those that are higher up within the company. These are relatively complex and can change or augment the overall direction and strategy of the company (Higher Bitesize Business Management, n.d.). These are decisions that affect the whole business and everyone that is working in it. Strategic decisions are typically made in line with the company's mission statement, and deal with the growth of the company (MSG Management Study Guide, n.d.). While participating in the simulation, the class left the major decisions up to our leader who would be considered a high-level manager in business context. All final decisions were made by him. If our strategy was not producing the type of results we aimed for, he was the one to change things like pricing and deciding whether or not it was a good time to issue stock.

A tactical decision falls somewhere between long-term and short term. In comparison to strategic decisions, they have a lower complexity and are made by middle managers. They build off of strategic decisions and attempt to reach the goals outlined in the strategic decisions (Higher Bitesize Business Management, n.d.). A tactical decision can include deciding on channels of communication, how much time to allot on a given task, or acquisition of resources (Developing People Through Decision Making, n.d.). The simulation required us to make a few tactical decisions. Although all final decisions had to go through our manager, we were able to input our opinions and ideas in the product spreadsheet. We were able to make tactical decisions concerning things whether to add a new product.

Operational decisions revolve around daily operations of companies. They are made by lower level management and are not complex, as they concern company operations (Developing People Through Decision Making, n.d.). These decisions are routine and require little business judgement. Tasks like placing orders for materials are involved with this type of decision. As previously mentioned, we had to run our ideas by our manager for them to be implemented, but overall the rest of the class had the freedom to make the simple decisions in our own weekly drafts.

Reflection

How would you assess your performance this term throughout the course of the simulation? What opportunities for performance improvement do you see regarding your simulation experience? How do you plan to take advantage of these opportunities to generate positive outcomes within the simulation? Refer to your answers from the preceding questions to support your answer. Include literature as necessary.

At this point of the simulation, it is a good time to reflect on how things have been going. In my opinion, I believe that my performance has been average. I believe that if the leaders of the simulations had been clearer about what our objectives for each week were, my performance would have been better. Also, if I had taken more initiative and put forth more effort, performance would have been above average.

I feel as though there are several opportunities for improvement. One way for myself and the class as a whole to improve is to work on communication. Although our manager put forth a great deal of effort throughout the whole simulation and effectively communicated in the beginning, communication declined as the simulation progressed. The same is true for the rest of the class. No channels of communication were established which is detrimental when trying to keep everyone on the same page. Many of us were confused and unclear about what exactly our goals and objectives were. If the communication was better, I believe we could have done much better. I plan to take advantage of this opportunity by being more involved and speaking up.

Another area of improvement is the effort received from the class. Many of us, failed to submit spreadsheets and did not put in enough effort. This is in part a result of many of us being unsure of what we were supposed to be doing and what exactly our role was in the class. Myself and others putting in more effort combined with getting a better understanding of objectives would allow us to improve and have more positive outcomes.

Although there are areas that need improvement, I think that we have done well overall. Our manager has put in effort since the beginning and is the main reason for the class's success. If the rest of us begin getting more involved, I believe that we will be able to be much more successful in the weeks to come.

Table 1: Relevant Literature for additional reading

Area	Topic	Authors
1	Accounting	Mook (2013) Nobes (2014) Exploring Business (2016)
2	Communication	Doss, Glover, Goza, & Wigginton (2015) Hargie (2006) Anthony (2018)
3	Finance	Brigham & Ehrhardt (2016) Doss, Sumrall, & Jones (2012) Valencia College (n.d.)
4	Economics	Boyes (2012) Doss, Sumrall, McElreath, & Jones (2013) McConnell, Brue, & Flynn (2015) Hughes (2015)
5	Ethics and Decisions	Baura (2006) Goza (2013) Decision Types (2014)
6	Information and Intelligence Analysis	Doss, Henley, Gokaraju, McElreath, & He (2016) McElreath, et al., (2014) Intelligence Analysis (n.d.)
7	Law and Legal Studies	Emerson (2016) Glover & Doss (2017) What is Business Law? (n.d.)
8	Logistics and Operations	Ailawadi & Singh (2012) Christoper (2016) Doss, McElreath, (2018) Wood (1998)
8	Marketing and Advertising	Henley & Doss (2013) Wright (1999) Gleeson (2018)
9	Process Improvement	Doss, Goza, Tesiero, Gokaraju, & McElreath (2017) Doss, Tesiero, Gokaraju, McElreath, & Goza (2017) Zahran (1998) Reh (2017)
10	Project Management	Badiru (2012) Harned (2017) What Is Project Management? (n.d.)
11	Quality Management	Doss, et al., (2016) Doss & Kamery (2006) Ross (1999) Quality Management (2017)
12	Security Management	Cabric (2015) Tipton & Krause (2002) What Is Security Management? (n.d.)
13	Strategic Management	Doss, Guo, & Lee (2011) Morden (2007) How Has This Term Impacted Your Life? (n.d.)
14	Technology	Liu, Yang, He, Li, & Doss (2016) Rosenberg (1976) Ramey (2013)

Throughout the course and during our simulation, we had to refer to outside sources for information. These sources provided aid in making decisions. Management was a topic that was used in almost every aspect of the simulation. I used the following articles to ensure that I had a tight grasp on the concept: *What Is Project Management, Quality Management, What Is Security Management?,* and *How Has This Term Impacted Your Life?*. *Decision Types* was included because with any type of management, decisions will be made. The writing provided definitions for each type. The way a company functions in based on its operations. To provide information about operations, I added Wood's writings. For areas of communication, I referred to an article written by L. Anthony. In this article, the connection between communication and strategy was discussed. The technology written by Ramey covered technology in businesses, and I used it to get a better understanding of various channels of communication that a company can choose to use, like email. The article *Exploring Business* and articles written by Valencia College and C. Hughes dealt with accounting, economics, and finance, respectively. They are relevant to the course because any business that is making a profit will use these concepts. Reh's article about process improvement was added because with benchmarking, areas for improvement will be discovered. Marketing and advertising are both very big parts of any business. The article written by Gleeson discusses the roles they have in companies. Law is very important because companies could find themselves in lawsuits, which is why I included *What is Business Law*?

References

Ailawadi, P. & Singh, R.P. (2012). *Logistics management*. (2nd). New Delhi, India: PHI Learning.
Anthony, L. (2018, January 31). Effective Communication & Leadership. Retrieved March 22, 2018, from http://smallbusiness.chron.com/effective-communication-leadership-5090.html
Badiru, A. (2012). *Project management: Systems, principles, and applications*. Boca Raton, FL: CRC Press.
Baura, G. (2006). *Engineering ethics: An industrial perspective*. Burlington, MA: Elsevier.
Boyes, W. (2012). *Managerial economics: Markets and the firm*. Mason, OH: South-Western.
Brigham, E. F. & Ehrhardt, M. C. (2017). *Financial management: Theory and practice*. (15th ed.). Boston, MA: Cengage.
Cabric, M. (2015). *Corporate security management: Challenges, risks, and strategies*. Waltham, MA: Butterworth-Heinemann.
Christopher, M. (2016). *Logistics & supply chain management*. New York, NY: Pearson.
Decision Types: 6 Types of Decisions Every Organization Need To Take. (2014, February 13). Retrieved March 22, 2018, from http://www.yourarticlelibrary.com/decision-making/decision-types-6-types-of-decisions-every-organization-need-to-take/25660
Developing people through decision-makingA npower case study. (n.d.). Retrieved March 22, 2018, from http://businesscasestudies.co.uk/npower/developing-people-through-decision-making/tactical-decisions.html
Doss, D., Glover, W., Goza, R., & Wigginton, M. (2015). *The foundations of communication in criminal justice systems*. Boca Raton, FL: CRC Press.
Doss, D., Goza, R., Tesiero, R., Gokaraju, B., & McElreath, D. (2017). The Capability Maturity Model as an industrial process improvement model. *Manufacturing Science and Technology, 4*(2), 17-24.
Doss, D., Guo, C, & Lee, J. (2011). *The business of criminal justice: A guide for theory and practice*. Boca Raton, FL: CRC Press.
Doss, D., Henley, R., Gokaraju, B., McElreath, D., & He, F. (2016). Integrating the GOMS model and the intelligence cycle. Journal of Business and Economics, 7(8), 1260-1268.
Doss, D., McElreath, D., Goza, R., Tesiero, R., Gokaraju, B., & Henley, R. (2018). Assessing the recovery aftermaths of selected disasters in the Gulf of Mexico. *Logistics & Sustainable Transport, 9*(1), 1-10.
Doss, D., McElreath, D., Jensen, C., Wigginton, M., Goza, R. Becker, U., & Roberts, R. (2016). *Management and administration for criminal justice organizations*. Dubuque, IA: Kendall-Hunt.
Doss, D., Sumrall, W., & Jones, D. (2012). *Strategic finance for criminal justice organizations*. Boca Raton, FL: CRC Press.
Doss, D., Sumrall, W., McElreath, D., & Jones, D. (2013). *Economic and financial analysis for criminal justice organizations*. Boca Raton, FL: CRC Press.
Doss, D., Tesiero, R., Gokaraju, B., McElreath, D., & Goza, R. (2017). Proposed derivation of the Integrated Capability Maturity Model as an environmental management maturity model. *Energy and Environmental Engineering, 5*(3), 67-73.
Doss, D.A. & Kamery, R. (2006). Exploring Total Quality Management (TQM) and derivative frameworks of the Capability Maturity Model (CMM). *Academy of Educational Leadership, 11*(1), 131.
Emerson, R. W. (2016). *Business law*. (6th ed.). Hauppage, NY: Barron's.
Exploring Business. (2016, April 08). Retrieved March 22, 2018, from http://open.lib.umn.edu/exploringbusiness/chapter/12-1-the-role-of-accounting/
Ghanbari, M. (2014, June 16). Business Goals vs. Objectives vs. Strategies vs. Tactics. Retrieved March 22, 2018, from https://www.linkedin.com/pulse/20140616055721-142774715-business-goals-vs-objectives-vs-strategies-vs-tactics/
Gleeson, P., Ph. D. (2018, March 15). The Importance of Marketing for the Success of a Business. Retrieved March 22, 2018, from http://smallbusiness.chron.com/importance-marketing-success-business-589.html
Glover, W. & Doss, D. (2017). *Business law for people in business*. Austin, TX: Sentia Publishing.
Goza, R. (2013). The ethics of record destruction. *Journal of Management Policy and Practice, 14*(6), 107.
Hargie, O. (2006). *The handbook of communication skills*. New York, NY: Routledge.
Harned, B. (2017). *Project management for humans: Helping people get things done*. Brooklyn, NY: Rosenfeld.
Henley, R. & Doss, D. (2013). B-to-B, Technology commercialization, & new product development. *Advances in Marketing, 2013*, 111.

Higher Bitesize Business Management - Decision-making in business : Revision. (n.d.). Retrieved March 22, 2018, from http://www.bbc.co.uk/bitesize/higher/business_management/business_enterprise/decision_making_business/revision/1/

How has this term impacted your life? (n.d.). Retrieved March 22, 2018, from http://www.businessdictionary.com/definition/strategy.html

Hughes, C. (2015, August 25). Business vs. economics: What is the difference? Retrieved March 22, 2018, from https://www.unigo.com/in-college/college-experience/business-vs-economics-what-is-the-difference

Intelligence analysis | Customized intelligence analysis services. (n.d.). Retrieved March 22, 2018, from https://assolution.com/services/intelligenceanalysis/

Liu, M., Yang, D., He, F., Li, M., & Doss, D. (2016). Perspectives of technology and the instrumentalist paradigm. *Proceedings of the Academy of Organizational Culture, Communications, and Conflict, 21*(1), 34-38.

McConnell, C., Brue, S., & Flynn, S. (2015). *Microeconomics*. (20th ed.). New York, NY: McGraw-Hill.

McElreath, D., Jensen, C., Wigginton, M., Doss, D., Nations, R. & Van Slyke, J. (2014). *Introduction to homeland security* (2nd ed.). Boca Raton, FL: CRC Press

Merchant, K. A. (n.d.). The Control Function of Management. Retrieved March 22, 2018, from https://sloanreview.mit.edu/article/the-control-function-of-management/

Mook, L. (2013). *Accounting for social value*. Toronto, Canada: University of Toronto Press.

Morden, T. (2007). *Principles of strategic management*. New York, NY: Routledge.

Morrison, M. (2011, September 29). Difference between goals and objectives. Retrieved March 22, 2018, from https://rapidbi.com/the-difference-between-goals-objectives/

MSG Management Study Guide. (n.d.). Retrieved March 22, 2018, from https://www.managementstudyguide.com/strategic-decisions.htm

Nobes, C. (2014). *Accounting: A very short introduction*. Oxford, UK: Oxford University Press.

Principles of Management. (2015, October 27). Retrieved March 22, 2018, from http://open.lib.umn.edu/principlesmanagement/chapter/1-5-planning-organizing-leading-and-controlling-2/

Principles of Management. (n.d.). Retrieved March 22, 2018, from https://courses.lumenlearning.com/suny-principlesmanagement/chapter/primary-functions-of-management/

Quality Management. (2017, November 20). Retrieved March 22, 2018, from https://www.investopedia.com/terms/q/quality-management.asp

Ramey, K. (2013, May 24). Use of Technology in Business Communication. Retrieved March 22, 2018, from https://www.useoftechnology.com/technology-business-communication/

Reh, F. J. (2017, March 31). Why Benchmarking is Important for Your Business and How to Get Started. Retrieved March 22, 2018, from https://www.thebalance.com/overview-and-examples-of-benchmarking-in-business-2275114

Riley, J. (n.d.). What is Strategy? | tutor2u Business. Retrieved March 22, 2018, from https://www.tutor2u.net/business/reference/what-is-strategy

Rosenberg, N. (1976). *Perspectives on technology*. New York, NY: Cambridge University Press.

Ross, J. (1999). *Total Quality Management: Text, cases, and readings*. (3rd ed.). Boca Raton, FL: CRC Press.

Tipton, H. & Krause, M. (2002). *Information security management handbook*. (4th). Boca Raton, FL: Auerbach Publications.

Valencia College. (n.d.). Retrieved March 22, 2018, from http://faculty.valenciacollege.edu/srusso/ch19bus.htm

What is Business Law? -. (n.d.). Retrieved March 22, 2018, from http://legalcareerpath.com/what-is-business-law/

What is corporate management? definition and meaning. (n.d.). Retrieved March 22, 2018, from http://www.businessdictionary.com/definition/corporate-management.html

What Is Project Management? (n.d.). Retrieved March 22, 2018, from https://www.pmi.org/about/learn-about-pmi/what-is-project-management

What Is Security Management? (n.d.). Retrieved March 22, 2018, from https://learn.org/articles/What_is_Security_Management.html

Wood, D. F. (1998, September 08). Logistics. Retrieved March 22, 2018, from https://www.britannica.com/topic/logistics-business

Wright, R. (1999). *Marketing, origins, concepts, environment*. London, UK: Thomson.

Zahran, S. (1998). *Software process improvement: Practical guidelines for business success*. New York, NY: Addison-Wesley.

YOUR KNOWLEDGE HAS VALUE

- We will publish your bachelor's and master's thesis, essays and papers

- Your own eBook and book - sold worldwide in all relevant shops

- Earn money with each sale

Upload your text at www.GRIN.com
and publish for free